Connecting

with Our Pets

in Heaven

Interpret Signs from Animals in the Afterlife, Cope with Grief, and Heal

Desha Utsick

Connecting
with Our Pets
in Heaven

Interpret Signs from Animals in the Afterlife, Cope with Grief, and Heal

Desha Utsick

Skyhorse Publishing

Skyhorse Publishing books may be purchased in bulk at special discounts for sales promotion, corporate gifts, fund-raising, or educational purposes. Special editions can also be created to specifications. For details, contact the Special Sales Department, Skyhorse Publishing, 307 West 36th Street, 11th Floor, New York, NY 10018 or info@skyhorsepublishing.com.

Skyhorse® and Skyhorse Publishing® are registered trademarks of Skyhorse Publishing, Inc.®, a Delaware corporation.

Visit our website at www.skyhorsepublishing.com.

10 9 8 7 6 5 4 3 2 1

Library of Congress Cataloging-in-Publication Data is available on file.

Design by Melissa Gerber
Images used under license by Shutterstock.com

Print ISBN: 978-1-5107-6700-3
Ebook ISBN: 978-1-5107-7176-5

Printed in China

Blessed are those who mourn,
for they will be comforted.

—Matthew 5:4

Contents

Approaching *the* Bridge

An Unbreakable Bond

CONNECTION • LOVE • LESSONS • PURPOSE

THE STRENGTH OF THE HUMAN-PET CONNECTION IS AMAZING. While we hear dramatic stories of animals rescuing their owners or even complete strangers from all sorts of physical peril, it's often the quiet moments spent in our day-to-day relationships with our animals that touch our lives the most and change us as people.

Pets remind us to slow down and value relationships. They highlight the importance of physical touch and unspoken communication. They model unconditional love and forgiveness. We grow together as we discover the significance of putting someone else first in our lives.

Whenever a pet comes into our lives, the encounter feels designed for a greater purpose. I know this was true of my rescue dog, Bella. On the outside, she appeared to need me more than I needed her. When our paths crossed, Bella wasn't in a good place. Extremely malnourished and skittish due to neglect and suspected abuse, she was close to being euthanized. But something called to me to rescue her. Little did I know, she would also rescue me—standing by my side through an addiction recovery process (that's another whole book!). Bella walked many miles by my side—literally and emotionally—as we explored nature and bared our souls to find a true path. She would grow into a strong presence whose thick black fur often caused her to be mistaken for a bear cub on hiking trails. She would share her gentle soul with anyone who needed a perky ear to listen and soft fur to stroke. She became somewhat of a celebrity everywhere we went and inspired us to be what she believed we all could be—people who look out for those with the least and those in the most need of our love.

Healing won't come overnight. What keeps
me strong and focused on my purpose in
this life is knowing that I am not alone.
Bella touched many lives with her presence,
and that doesn't just fade away.

Losing Bella in 2020 was devastating for me. She was ready to be at physical peace, but that didn't make the decisions or experience any easier. After she passed, daily routines that had become so meaningful were shaken. Life seemed unsteady and too quiet. When it all felt too overwhelming, I would think about Bella and her strength. She would lend me whatever I needed to get through. I could turn to all I had experienced in the moments we spent together and what she had taught me in this life.

A year later, finding ways to get through each day without my Bella physically by my side is still a constant journey. After all, grieving is a normal, healthy process; healing won't come overnight. What keeps me strong and focused on my purpose in this life is knowing that I am not alone. Bella touched many lives with her presence, and that doesn't just fade away. Love for her and from her is still very much alive in all who knew her. Others who have

lost their own beloved pets are with me in my grief, transition, and healing. God is with me, letting me know I am loved and cherished. Bella is with me— just in a new way.

Any change is difficult, and loss of a loved one can be downright devastating. As our pets cross what some call the rainbow bridge, it can be especially challenging to stretch our faith and see how pets can remain an integral part of our lives. I have come to a point where I experience Bella all the time as I go through ordinary and also trying days. Her presence brings me peace, perspective, and patience and serves as a reminder of all I can do in this life while looking forward to being reunited with her in a place of eternal love one day. With all of the blessings pets bring into our lives, why wouldn't they be part of that glory? Why wouldn't that connection live on?

Our bonds with our pets go far beyond the physical relationship to reach the

If we can lean into the
strength of that love
and the lessons we have
gathered, our days remain
blessed even when our
pets leave this world.

depths of our minds, hearts, and souls. If we can lean into the strength of that love and the lessons we have gathered, our days remain blessed even when our pets leave this world and cross that rainbow bridge. This hope, this strength, this healing through a time of grief are what I hope you take away from this book. Open your heart to the signs from heaven that are around you every day!

Getting Through Grief

EMOTIONS • MEMORIES • SPACE • STAGES

♥

IT WOULD BE WONDERFUL TO SAY THAT WE REACH A PLACE OF
HOPE AND UNDERSTANDING OVERNIGHT. But that wouldn't be true
or helpful to suggest. When we lose a beloved companion, it can take time to
make it through the grief. We may second-guess everything, wondering if we
did all we could. We may even blame ourselves. We may question our relationship. We may question our beliefs. These are all normal reactions as we process
the experience.

The wording here is so important: We don't get "over" grief, we get
"through" it. Because it's only when we try to avoid it or imagine it away that
it tends to grow bigger and more uncrossable. Although the pain of loss can
often feel overwhelming and can trigger all sorts of tough emotions, we need to
remember that's it OK, even healthy, to grieve loss in our lives.

So often, grief for pets gets minimized—and that's unfortunate. While
some people may not understand the relationship we shared with a special pet,
we should never feel guilty or ashamed about grieving for an animal. Seeing
pets as God's beloved creations and members of our family is truly a blessing.
The depth of our love is what makes the loss so tough. The depth of our love
says something important about us as people and how we value relationships.

What also complicates matters is that grief looks different for everyone.
Grieving is a highly individualized experience, based on our experiences, the
circumstances of our pet's life and death, our personal beliefs, and our natural
emotional tendencies. For one person, grief may be expressed through tearful
outbursts, while another expresses grief through verbal processing—everything
from sharing countless stories to questioning why it had to happen the way it
did. What brings healing may vary, but paths through the grief often include:

Emotional release. It's OK to cry and show outward signs of grief for our loved ones. Our bonds are very strong, and for many of us the loss is felt so deeply that it cannot be put into words.

Sharing memories. Find people with whom you can talk about your loved one. Talk about the good times but also the challenges, and even the way it ended if that's what you need to do. Sharing memories is instrumental in the grieving process and can help us move toward healing.

The depth of our love is what makes the loss so tough. The depth of our love says something important about us as people and how we value relationships.

Celebrating life. Memorial services for our loved ones can be very healing. They will look different for each person. Some may bury their pets, while others scatter their ashes in a favorite place. Gathering, remembering, and even praying as a community can be powerful. It's a great way to recall wonderful memories while enjoying support in the presence of those you love.

Honoring your pet through giving. Consider what you could do in your pet's honor—such as donating to an animal charity, volunteering at a local animal shelter, or pet sitting a friend's loved one.

Most of all, give yourself the gift of time and space as you grieve. Perhaps you've heard of the Kübler-Ross model, more commonly known as the five stages of grieving: denial, anger, bargaining, depression, and acceptance. Entire books could be written on each stage! But the following are the most important points to take to heart based on this research of how we go through the universal process of grieving:

Grief is normal. The loss of any relationship needs to be mourned. Practice patience and forgiveness for yourself. Remember that our animal friends move past grief and other afflictions with greater poise than we humans can ever do.

There is no time frame or limit for our grief. The Kübler-Ross model isn't linear or all-inclusive. Not everyone will experience all five stages, and you may not go through them in this order. These stages are simply tools to help us understand and identify how we feel. Know that there will be steps, but let your heart reveal what it needs and when it's ready for your personal next step.

There is something else that I didn't realize until researching and writing this book. It is suggested that we go through four tasks of mourning, as described by J. William Worden in his book *Grief Counselling and Grief Therapy*. The first task is to accept the reality of the loss. The second is to walk through the pain of the grief. Task number three is to adjust to an environment in which the deceased is missing, and the fourth task is to find an enduring connection with the deceased while embarking on a new life.

Again, they are not in any particular order; we may need to revisit certain tasks over time. Not aiming to define right and wrong approaches, these models are designed to help us understand and identify a little more of what we are experiencing. Knowing that we are not alone in what we are going through is so important and healing! But what probably excited me the most was that fourth task.

So, how do we find an enduring connection with our beloved companion while embarking on a new life in the here and now? We watch for, listen for, and experience signs from heaven in our everyday lives.

Finding Hope in Signs

COMFORT · INSIGHT · PRESENCE · HEALING

MEMORIES OF OUR PETS CAN BRING BOTH JOY AND SADNESS, ESPECIALLY IN THE BEGINNING OF OUR GRIEVING PERIOD. We remember the great times we shared together, but we still long for them to be back with us. We are blessed to have had them in our lives, but it's never really long enough, is it?

We've watched our pets learn and grow. We've watched them play and rest. We've watched them make their way through this big world of ours. We've watched them struggle through aging or an illness or injury.

When they leave us and make their transition onward, we are left with a loud silence and void that cannot be ignored. They are at peace, but we are left behind, missing them so much. Their work is done here, but ours isn't. So we must press on, knowing through faith that they are more than OK.

In fact, if we are open to receiving them, we will see or hear or feel signs that our loved ones are whole again, joyous and free in a new life. We can find comfort and hope through these signs, knowing they are in the best place ever, waiting to greet us when it's our time to join them.

The type of signs you experience may be based on special moments shared with your pet in this life. For me, rainbows seemed to follow us wherever we went. I always feel Bella reaching out when I see the bright colors. (You can read about one of my rainbow experiences on page 80.) Sometimes, the signs we experience are connected to what we need in the moment—a sense of peace through an eagle soaring above, rest and comfort through the warmth of a sunbeam, a nudge from a butterfly to let us know something new and beautiful is about to enter our lives.

Sometimes, the signs we experience are connected to what we need in the moment—a nudge from a butterfly to let us know something new and beautiful is about to enter our lives.

Signs may appear in our daily lives or in our dreams. Aimee C. shares how dreams helped her family move toward healing after the passing of their dog:

"Our pug, Meatball, was a happy, chubby family dog with thick black fur, a curly tail, and loads of personality. My two sons grew up chasing him around the backyard, snuggling with him as they watched their favorite cartoons, reading to him before bed, and laughing at his old-man snores. They were preteens by the time he passed away. He was just a little dog, but he left a giant hole in our lives. I'd been saying goodbye to Meatball for the span of a year, watching his lungs begin to fail and his joy for life recede, so I had readied myself for his death. The kids, who lived only in the moment, felt it all at once.

When I surprised my children months later with Scoot the Golden Retriever pup, the kids were excited, but torn. My oldest was concerned that it was a betrayal of Meatball to love another dog so soon. He kept his distance as best as he could, feeling like he owed Meatball as much. My youngest was less able to resist the furry charms of a galloping, Golden puppy, but he would confide in me at night that he felt guilty every time Scoot slept where Meatball used to lay, at the foot of his bed. I assured my kids that Meatball would want them to let go, but they were unconvinced.

Several nights later, both boys came downstairs to breakfast announcing that they'd had the most realistic dream. One at a time, they explained that Meatball had visited them in the night. Shocked that they had both dreamt about Meatball the same night, we listened as my youngest explained that in his dream, Meatball had seen Scoot on his bed and had snuggled up next to him and gone to sleep. For my oldest, the dream was him scooping up his old friend to hug and kiss him as much as he liked. I felt a surge of gratitude to Meatball for releasing my kids from their guilt and for continuing to care for them as he had when he was alive. Their hearts seemed to open up after that night of dreams and, with Meatball's blessing, they were able to accept a new puppy into their lives."

"One at a time, they explained that Meatball had visited them in the night. . . . I felt a surge of gratitude to Meatball for releasing my kids from their guilt and for continuing to care for them as he had when he was alive."

Robyn G. also received a pet message through a dream:

"When I was about two years old, our neighbors' dog had puppies. Just a few weeks later, one of those puppies started digging under the fence every day to play with me and my sister. We, of course, fell in love with him. My mother jokingly said, 'If he crawls under there one more time, I'm not giving him back!' The next day, like clockwork, we went out to play and the black ball of fluff wriggled his way under the fence to join us. When my mother went to return him, I threw a toddler hissy fit. 'You pwomised!' And that's how Fluffy joined our family. We considered him our brother/son and spoiled him for almost fifteen years until he passed.

Fast forward another ten years and my parents were empty nesters. I'm pretty sure they still felt the hole Fluffy left more keenly than the recent absence of their children. Then one night, I had a dream that Fluffy was in our old yard as if no time has passed. He looked at me and I heard the words, 'It's time. They're ready for your new brother.' I woke up feeling a mixture of sadness and excitement. I still missed him after all those years but was happy that they were ready to love again.

I called my mother to tell her this wonderful and moving experience I had. She laughed. I mean, the dog talked! I couldn't exactly blame her. About a week later, I got a voicemail from my mother asking me to call her back. Despite her casual tone, I just knew the reason for the call. I called her back and when she answered, I didn't even say hello. 'You got a dog, didn't you?!' I yelled, more as a statement than a question. She just laughed and asked how I knew. It had been an impulse adoption as they walked past a rescue that was at a flea market. Maybe she thought it was an impulse, but I knew she had been ready. I heard it from an old friend."

In our daily lives, we may be more attuned to signs that connect with our strongest senses. I am a photographer at heart, so it never surprises me that scenes capture me more than sounds or feelings. If you have a dominant sense that guides the way you interact with the world, you may experience stronger connections with your pet or with God through this sense. Lean into it.

Sometimes the signs are very obvious (like that rainbow or eagle), but other times signs from heaven can be more subtle—like encountering peaceful waters or a feeling of warmth or presence. You'll find stories of all sorts of experiences in the A-to-Z Signs from Heaven section that makes up most of this book. No matter which stories you connect with most or which signs you experience for yourself, you'll begin to see (if you haven't already) that our pets never truly leave us. They leave imprints on our hearts and their marks and presence all through our lives. You'll also find that our God never leaves us. He helps us to experience the love and bond with our pets that we felt so strongly in this life in a new, eternal way. And that's because He is always with us and sees the pain and grief we experience. He reaches out with comfort all the time; we just need to be aware of all the marvelous ways in which He can work. Any sign from the spiritual realm is important and has a purpose for us, the recipients.

The timing in which we receive a sign can be a miracle in itself. Kathy W. shares how she received a message of comfort just when she needed it:

> "About four years ago, I was cleaning out a huge storage room of my belongings with a close girlfriend. It was a massive undertaking. My hands gingerly came across the wicker box that contained my cat Missy's old toys, her pawprint in clay, and her paperwork from the day she went to heaven. (I still have her ashes at home.) So I said, 'Ahhh, look! Here are all of Missy's things that I packed away years ago!' I opened up the box with tears in my eyes and read the poem the vet gave to me on March 16, 2012, the day she passed. Suddenly, my friend and I realized . . . '*Today* is March 16!' I cried like a baby. I truly believe it was Missy letting me know that she's still by my side. She was an extraordinary cat. Smart as a whip and a sweet companion for almost 20 years."

When I lost my special girl Bella, it felt like a part of me was lost with her. But I have seen signs from God and her that have brought me back to life and myself. I have been comforted by them tremendously. In the process of sharing stories with other pet lovers, I've found that I am not alone in that experience. Many people have shared sights, sounds, or sometimes just a strong sense of "knowing" that their pet's love is surrounding them, that their pet is at peace, that their pet has sent them a message that it's time to welcome a new animal to the family. In some inexplicable way that we can only chalk up to faith, our pets are still very much a part of our journeys.

All sorts of comforts and communications can come through when we're open. Once we become aware and intuitive, we will see them. Get ready for it to be healing and life-changing!

A-to-Z Signs
from Heaven

Butterflies

TRANSFORMATION · REBIRTH · GROWTH · HOPE

SEEING A BUTTERFLY FLUTTERING THROUGH THE SKY OR HOVERING AROUND A FLOWER BRINGS US A SENSE OF PEACE, HOPE, AND BEAUTY, OF COURSE. We associate butterflies with sunny weather and cheery seasons. But the sight can also take us much deeper into opportunities for growth if we consider how a butterfly has come into maturation and how far a butterfly may have come to cross our path.

The entire transformation from caterpillar to butterfly may take anywhere from one month to two years, depending on the type of butterfly. In all cases, the time is made up of four developmental stages—all with unique goals to help growth. We can take this fact as a lesson in our own lives. In time, which varies for everyone, we too can be transformed stage by stage, and something beautiful can come of even the toughest experiences if we're open to watching, learning, and accepting opportunities for a kind of rebirth or coming out of our cocoons. In particular, the sudden sight of a butterfly after a pet has left this world can remind us that even though a stage of physical connection with our pet has ended, all that we've been through together has helped us grow and prepare for something new that could be waiting just around the corner.

"I wished [Missy] could be there with me again—that I could feel the weight of her on my lap and her soft fur tickling my arms—and I started to cry. At that exact moment, a butterfly landed in my lap."

Linda S. felt a sense of hope and connection when a butterfly landed in her life after losing her cat companion:

> "My cat, Missy, was obsessed with butterflies. We'd put on her harness and lead and take her butterfly 'hunting' in the backyard. I never let her catch one, of course, but she loved to bound all over the garden after them. When she got tired, we'd just sit in the sunny spot on the bench, Missy in my lap, and watch them flutter around.
>
> After Missy passed, I found myself spending a lot of time in that garden. I would just sit quietly, watching the butterflies and feeling the sun on my face. One day in particular, I seemed to be missing her more than usual. I wished she could be there with me again—that I could feel the weight of her on my lap and her soft fur tickling my arms—and I started to cry. At that exact moment, a butterfly landed in my lap. It sat there for a long minute before finally fluttering off to explore some marigolds. I knew it was Missy in some unexplainable way."

What was Missy trying to communicate? The lightness of a butterfly's being reminds us not to allow burdens and losses to weigh us down forever. There is always a new stage waiting when we've given ourselves a healthy time to grieve and we're ready for growth. Change isn't an easy thing for most of us, but we may find unexpected beauty in the journey—even through grief. Think about what new developments in your life might be ready to take flight—now or in a season.

Cardinals

VITALITY • LOVE • DEVOTION • FREEDOM

OF ALL THE SPIRITUAL SIGNS WE MAY EXPERIENCE AFTER A LOVED ONE LEAVES THIS PHYSICAL WORLD, SEEING A CARDINAL IS PROBABLY ONE OF THE MOST COMMON. Chances are, you've heard someone share a cardinal sighting and connect it to a loved one they've lost. Many people consider these bright birds to be spiritual messengers that have been sent by our loved ones in heaven to watch over us.

In fact, cardinals have been steeped in spiritual traditions and beliefs for a long time. Consider the title of cardinal in the Catholic Church and the bright red robe he wears. In Native American cultures, cardinals are often associated with the sun and seen as carriers of good luck and vitality in a sense beyond the physical. Because they are often spotted in pairs, cardinals can spark a sense of strong devotion and eternal bonds as well.

Birds in general tend to signify freedom. Seeing a cardinal may be a loved one's way of communicating that they have found freedom from the earthly realm and are sending a message that we can release any concerns.

"I'd never seen so many [cardinals] at once—females and males, flitting through the branches but staying put in the tree. I just knew that Sally had sent them to me."

Jeff B. feels that his horse shared a message as bold as her life on earth:

> "I had this stubborn, strong-willed, redheaded mare named Sally who absolutely hated being ridden in the paddock. She just threw fits until we went out on the trails. After one good gallop, Sally would relax and actually let me enjoy the ride.
>
> We'd walk around the big field and into the woods, seeing if we could spot new birds along the way. We had seen all sorts of birds, from mockingbirds to woodpeckers and even the occasional hawk. But my favorites were the bright red cardinals. It was always a good day when we caught a flash of red in a tree.
>
> The day after I lost Sally, I opened up the barn doors that led out to the back paddock like I always do. But this time, I found that the big oak tree out back was absolutely full of cardinals. I'd never seen so many at once—females and males, flitting through the branches but staying put in the tree. I just knew that Sally had sent them to me."

In that moment, Sally let Jeff know that she was stronger than ever and their connection was still strong as well. He could feel at peace remembering the times they had together and understanding that she was experiencing a new world that he, too, would see one day—a tree full of life.

Clouds

DIVINITY • HEAVEN • REVELATION • GIFT

THINK BACK TO WHEN YOU WERE A CHILD, LYING IN THE GRASS
AND WATCHING CLOUDS ROLL BY. What did you see or sense as you
watched wisps, puffs, or almost magical formations? As we move into adult-
hood, we often forget to simply pause and look up. But the clouds are still there,
waiting for us to discover their messages.

Clouds can act as signs in two ways. First, they may simply impart a strong
feeling. So, we may appreciate how quickly a dark cloud can pass and uncover
the sun again, just as time and circumstances pass in our lives and we feel
warmth again after a dark or lonely spell—as can often be felt in grief. Clouds
may also reveal shapes and formations that lead to meaning. We may see a
smiley face, prompting us to smile ourselves. Or we may see a heart that leads
us to feel loved. (For a deeper discussion, see Hearts, beginning on page 52.) In
either case, clouds are often associated with the divine, and it's easy to see how
messages can be received as heaven-sent.

Barbara C.'s sign from heaven was *very* clear—its appearance and its significance:

> "My baby, Minnie, and I loved to go on walks together. It was our time to ourselves away from all the stresses and noise of life. Toward the end, she had a hard time walking, so I bought one of those pet strollers and pushed her around the neighborhood. You could see her eyes just drinking everything in, her little tail wagging every time a squirrel ran by or a person stopped to say hello.
>
> I kept taking our walks after she passed just to feel close to her. And every day, I would wish for a sign that she made it across the rainbow bridge. About a week later, I got that sign. It was an overcast day with gray and white swirls of clouds hanging low in the sky. And there among them was Minnie's face. I know how crazy that sounds, but this wasn't a puff of white that sort of resembled a dog. It was like a painting of her face taken from my favorite picture of her. Minnie was telling me she made it to heaven."

Because what we sense or see in clouds can vary so much, we need to be alert and receptive to messages intended for us. As Barbara discovered, cloud formations are tailored specifically for each of us and each of our needs at the very moment we see them. And, wow, how they can speak to us—it's hard to deny what's written in the skies! Simply looking up will also remind us of how much our pets are a gift from heaven, and that they are gifted with heaven now.

"I kept taking our walks after [Minnie] passed just to feel close to her. And every day, I would wish for a sign that she made it across the rainbow bridge. About a week later, I got that sign."

Eagles

FREEDOM • COURAGE • RELEASE • INSPIRATION

CATCHING A GLIMPSE OF AN EAGLE IS A SPECIAL, BLESSED MOMENT. We are reminded of just how majestic eagles are as they spread their wings, and how confident and in control they look as they rest. Even from a distance, the sight can make us stop in our tracks and take in its natural beauty. And when we pause, what do we feel?

When an eagle grabs our attention, we may see it as a way our beloved companion is reaching out to us and sending us a reminder that they are now truly free. We no longer need to feel conflicted, as there is peace and power in the message. Seeing an eagle can be an answer to a prayer or a completely unexpected encounter. Either way, it's usually just what we need in the moment and a great reminder of the bigger picture—that our loved ones who have passed on are more than OK, soaring high with a sense of release from any burdens they bore in this life.

Sandy B. shares her experience with seeing an eagle after her dog passed on:

> "My first English bull terrier, Jessie, was my heart dog. She saved me
> from extreme depression after my samoyed, Sammy, passed away. I was
> so despondent that my husband, not one to do this type of thing, picked
> up the phone and made arrangements with a breeder for us to visit with
> their puppies. It turned out that those puppies were born the day my
> Sammy died. That alone sent chills down my arms. I knew the one white
> girl they had was meant to be ours! Turned out she was *mine*.
>
> I called her my angel because she saved me. We spent nearly sixteen
> years (one month shy) together. She was my heart and soul. Although we
> had two other dogs, she was my 'best girl.' When her time to leave my
> world came and I let her go, I was at such a loss, even though I still had
> two dogs to care for. She passed in March of that year, and we were at
> the end of May with no sign from her. I was devastated.
>
> The end of May brought Memorial Day weekend, and the twice-
> yearly worship service on the beach in our lake community. It was a
> gorgeous day, and as the pastor spoke and his wife played guitar, I asked
> God for a sign that my beloved Jessie was OK and that she was with
> Him. No sooner had the lightly whispered prayer left my lips than an
> eagle flew by, low along the horizon in front of me, over the lake. Again
> the chills came and I began to silently cry with joy, knowing this was my
> heaven-sent sign."

Sandy's eagle sighting brought her great comfort and confidence that there is a
place of peace waiting for all of us, including our pets. Eagles are often seen as
signs of inspiration, courage, strength, freedom, victory, release from bondage,
immortality, and even resurrection as they rise and soar through the skies.
In fact, they are considered the "kings of the skies" that can carry powerful
messages to our head and heart.

"I asked God for a sign that my beloved Jessie was OK and that she was with Him. No sooner had the lightly whispered prayer left my lips than an eagle flew by."

Feathers

LOVE · COMFORT · PROTECTION · ENCOURAGEMENT

IF YOU FIND FEATHERS, ESPECIALLY WHITE ONES, AFTER A LOVED ONE HAS PASSED, TAKE COMFORT. Feathers are believed by many to be a form of communication from the deceased and also are viewed as an angelic message of love, protection, and encouragement to those left behind. We may find them in spots our pets considered special, or they may suddenly appear to us anywhere, anytime we feel lost in grief.

Anna R. welcomed the sight of white feathers as a comfort in her grief when she lost her dog companion:

> "Long before she got to heaven, I called my Lucy a 'guardian angel.' She was there for me after my divorce and helped me get to the other side. Walking with her got me out of the house; snuggling with her helped lift my spirits. She even took up the empty side of the bed. By the time she passed, Lucy had helped me through so much. I was heartbroken to lose her, but I was in a better place to deal with the loss because of her.
>
> Now, if you've ever seen an Irish Red and White Setter, you know that they have these gorgeous white 'feathers' all over. Whenever I would get lost in thought or grief, I would find myself just absentmindedly stroking those soft feathers. Lucy never seemed to mind. Well, ever since losing her, I've found actual downy white feathers in all of her favorite spots. I notice they'll pop up within hours of me thinking of her. I like to think it's her way of saying she's still watching over me."

"Ever since losing [Lucy], I've found actual downy white feathers in all of her favorite spots. . . . I like to think it's her way of saying she's still watching over me."

Kim B. also considers feathers a sign of care and comfort from her cat, whom she lost last year:

> "Sadie, like many cats, had two speeds: napping and running furiously through the house. When she was in that feisty mood, her favorite thing to do was 'attack' a cat toy consisting of a wand, string, and pretend mouse with feathers attached. We must have gone through ten of those wands in a year as she systematically detached the feathers and then the mouse. There would be nights I was tempted to put in more long work hours, but she would find me and wrap herself around my ankles, meowing and demanding wand playtime. Honestly, it was a healthy reminder to take a break and discover some simple joy. It's too easy to bury ourselves in to-do lists!
>
> Since Sadie crossed the rainbow bridge, I have found feathers in many different places in moments when I was beginning to feel my head explode with pressure. I know it's Sadie trying to protect me from falling into the time traps again. It's not always easy, but I try to heed her reminders, lighten my load, and engage in some human play."

Finding feathers can help us remember that in time the burden of loss we experience when a pet dies will be lighter. Feathers are also a reminder to seek joy and look on the lighter side of life whenever we can. In the scope of eternity, this moment is just a feather floating in the breeze.

"Since Sadie crossed the rainbow bridge, I have found feathers in many different places in moments when I was beginning to feel my head explode with pressure. I know it's Sadie trying to protect me."

Feeling of Presence

LOVE • COMFORT • PEACE • CONNECTION

MANY PET GUARDIANS REPORT SEEING, HEARING, SMELLING, OR FEELING THE PRESENCE OF THEIR LOVED ONE AFTER THE PET HAS PASSED. But sometimes it's even more difficult to describe in our human sensory terms. We may get a strong feeling of our loved ones being right by our side or passing by us. It can be hard to describe as anything more than a "knowing."

Feeling the presence of a pet may be a strong, undeniable feeling, or as light as a gentle whisper or a still, small voice. When we get this sense in any form that it comes, we feel comfort, realizing they truly are still with us in one sense, and yet knowing that they are in a place of great peace at the same time.

"Every so often, when I'm by the koi pond, I can feel [Twoey] there. I can't explain it, but I just know that he's choosing to be with me. . . . I try to be present with him in that moment."

Jane S. treasures the times when she feels the presence of her cat:

"Our cat, Twoey, was a character. He was a big black cat with a buddha belly and a scratchy meow like an old man who had smoked all his life. The first time we met him, Twoey walked right into the house, jumped up on the recliner, and went to sleep, belly up, like he'd lived with us all his life.

At the time, we already had a black cat named Midnight, and so did our neighbors. We just assumed he was the other Midnight (Midnight Two) and let him come and go as he pleased. A few weeks later, our neighbor stopped by to chat and saw Twoey circling our legs. She asked if we got another cat. My dad's eyes went wide as he said, 'Isn't this *your* cat?' She said no, hers was a skinny little girl. We realized we'd been adopted.

Twoey lived a long, happy life as an indoor-outdoor cat (there was no keeping him inside—he wouldn't have it). He never went far, though. You could usually find him drinking out of the koi pond. Twoey passed away from lymphoma a few years ago. But every so often, when I'm by the koi pond, I can feel him there. I can't explain it, but I just know that he's choosing to be with me. So I say hello, tell him that I love him, and just try to be present with him in that moment."

Colin C. has had a similar experience with his special dog in the northern woods of Maine:

"I've had many dogs over the years—all great dogs—yet one became a deeper part of me. Ruger was my first Labrador retriever, and I trained him to find moose and deer 'sheds.' Sheds are antlers that fall off every winter, and the deer and moose then grow a new set each year. Ruger and I have been in the most remote places in the entire US. Our bond was so strong that I still can't even put it into words. Together we have ventured into places that I haven't been to with another human. He trusted me, and I trusted him. The peace I felt deep within my soul having him along is something that will live inside me forever.

Ruger passed away in November 2019. After his passing, going into the woods without him physically by my side left a huge hole in me. I continue to get out, though, and I know he is always with me—just in a different way. I can feel him and even see him working gracefully.

Recently, I went up north in Maine to look for moose sheds. As I always do now, I wore my necklace that contains some of Ruger's ashes. I entered a beautiful area and so badly wanted Ruger with me. I talked to him out loud, and inside I sensed he could still hear me. That day, I found my first moose shed without him. Yet I felt he was there with me, looking at me with his big brown, loving eyes. He will always be with me, in my heart and spiritually."

No matter when our paths diverge with those of our pets, we remain connected through bonds that can't be broken. We walk together, even if it's difficult to explain how we know. We just know, and the feeling brings peace to our souls.

"I felt [Ruger] was there with me, looking at me with his big brown, loving eyes. He will always be with me, in my heart and spiritually."

Goose Bumps

ENERGY · PRESENCE · STRENGTH · AFFIRMATION

Brrr! We may experience goose bumps simply from chilly conditions, but just as often we feel goose bumps based on a strong emotional response. Because we become so bonded with our pets, it's not surprising that a certain memory of a pet or situation connected to a pet could trigger a goose bump response. Maybe it's touching the window control in the car if your special dog loved to stick his head out into the breeze. Or hearing a certain song that drove him to hilarious barking or howling that your family called "singing." Or opening that can of tuna that

would bring your beloved (hungry!) cat rushing to your feet (or jumping on the counter!).

So, is it just an emotional response or something more? When we're connected to a loved one, it's not unreasonable to feel connected to their energy—even when they've crossed the rainbow bridge. Feel something you simply can't explain? It could be a message from heaven. Pet owners who experience these moments of intensity say that the experience leaves them comforted by the presence of their pet, affirmed that their pet is OK and no longer suffering, and inspired or energized to take the next step in their journey through grief. Here is a beautiful example from Jonathan B:

> "My border collie, Maggie, was a retired working dog that I adopted when my friend sold her farm. She was incredibly loving and loyal, but that dog *needed* a job. If you didn't give her one, she'd find one on her own—and it might be herding your neighbor's kids when you're not looking.
>
> One day, I had an idea to call up the local sheep farm and ask if we could arrange a 'playdate.' Turned out, they were happy to have Maggie come teach their young border collie a thing or two. We started going every weekend, and Maggie started to relax in her time off. I always got goose bumps watching that dog work.
>
> After she died, I went back to the sheep farm to see how the other dog, Bo, was doing in his new role as alpha. I thought to myself as I watched him, 'He's great, but he's no Maggie.' Just as the thought crossed my mind, I felt goose bumps creep up my arms and down my back. And I knew she was there with me, giving me one of her appreciative nudges."

"I felt goose bumps creep up my arms and down my back. And I knew [Maggie] was there with me, giving me one of her appreciative nudges."

Kurt H. has experienced this phenomenon many times . . . all in one special place:

> "Annie was my first Boxer. My sweet Annie. I would take her out to Sand Spring Lake at Hickory Run State Park, her favorite place. She would get so excited when she knew we were going. When she passed, I took her ashes out there. I'll never forget it. When I released her ashes, a swirling wind took them up to the clouds. Every time I go there now, I get crazy goose bumps. I feel her big-time."

We may experience goose bumps during moments of intense emotion, extraordinary inspiration, or spiritual connection—or some combination of all of those. Embrace the energy and the message of comfort and strength your pet is sending you, letting you know they're OK and it may be time to move forward in healing your heart.

Hearts

LOVE • HOPE • LIFE ENERGY • ETERNITY

♡

SEEING A HEART CAN FILL US WITH WARMTH. We may think of Valentine's Day sentiments shared or someone communicating their love to us with a heart drawn near their name in a letter. We even sometimes make the heart symbol with our hands as an expression to others. One of the earliest symbols a child attempts to draw is a heart to share their feelings with family and friends.

But hearts leap beyond paper and our hands. Heart motifs often show up in nature—from part of a tree that has formed in a heart-shape knot or hollow to a weathered rock whose edges have softened and rounded into something resembling a heart. Clouds can appear in heart-like formations, as can individual leaves or piles of brush. Sunlight may stream to create heart-shaped sunspots or shadows.

The sight of a heart that appears almost mystically in our environment after a pet has left this world points to an eternal love. (True love never leaves us; it just transforms.) The discovery can fill us with hope and energy, knowing that our beloved companion is experiencing a new life—and we will too.

"When it was his time, it happened in our family room. . . . Almost in the exact spot where Laz left us, the grain in the wood forms a small heart."

Fran D. found an encouraging surprise when he decided to do a little remodeling:

"We had a big Lab named Lazarus. He lived to be about fourteen, but the last few years were rough on him. He was so bad that we could not get him to the vet, but the vet was nice enough to come to our house. When it was his time, it happened in our family room. Every time my wife walked over the spot, she would sigh and say his name. Fast-forward about a year and we decided to rip up the carpet and install wood flooring. Almost in the exact spot where Laz left us, the grain in the wood forms a small heart. It's not perfect, but it does look like a slightly misshapen heart. You know, it was not until I started sharing this story that I got the obvious connection between his name and the sign of his presence."

No matter where hearts appear in our comings and goings, we feel our own hearts rise and rejoice within us. If a heart appears to you, stop and say your special pet's name and know that the bond is forever between you. Your pet likely changed your heart in some great way and we receive reminders to hold on to that growth and take it even further into the world.

Introductions

HEALING • COMFORT • CONNECTION

ONE OF THE GREATEST GIFTS OUR PETS CAN GIVE US WHEN THEY LEAVE THIS WORLD IS TO CONNECT US TO EXPANDED LOVE. There are countless stories of beloved pets pointing their humans in a certain direction through a little divine intervention to help them find or be found by their next pet companion in life.

So if you're feeling a nudge toward an animal in need of a worthy home, pay attention. You may not think you're ready to bring another pet into the family, but you may get a pretty strong sign otherwise, as Lloyd S. did. Here's his story:

"Years ago, we had a one-of-a-kind dog that was part yellow Lab, part Husky, and part Chow. Casey was a wonderful, loving companion. When we saw Casey suffering at age fourteen, our son Jonathan was devastated. Casey had been his dog from day one, so Jonathan insisted on going with me to the vet. There, in the vet's office, Jonathan held his beloved dog in his arms while Casey quietly and painlessly went to sleep for the last time. As an act of kindness in a tough time, the vet told us not to bother stopping at the front desk to handle the costs, but to just come back in a few weeks when we felt we were ready to do so.

Fast-forward a few weeks, I went back to the vet to pay our bill. On the counter, in a tiny bed, was a yellow-orange tiger kitty. He was just a few days old. The vet tech explained that a neighbor of the vet had a cat that recently birthed a litter. All of the kittens had been adopted out but this little guy. He had a slight deformity to his one eyelid, which caused it to not fully open. Because he would need surgery, everyone passed

"It is often said that we don't choose
our animals; rather, they choose
us. This was certainly the case with
the kitty we named Sammy."

on him. The neighbor, the vet tech explained, needed to go out of town and asked the vet if he would board the kitten for a few days—even though the vet didn't board but only kept animals at the clinic while they recovered from procedures. As a favor to a longtime friend, the vet agreed to help. But now it had been three weeks with no scheduled pickup.

So here was me. And then here was this four-week-old little tiger kitty sleeping in his cute little bed each day under the warmth of a heat lamp on the front counter in the hopes of earning himself a forever home. To help, the vet was offering the needed eye surgery and neutering free. Can you guess the next part? When my wife, Sandy, came home from work that day, which happened to be a few days before her birthday, she found an animal carrier. Our new family member lightly cried out to make his presence known and announce that he'd like to be let out of his confounded confinement.

It is often said that we don't choose our animals; rather, they choose us. This was certainly the case with the kitty we named Sammy. Sammy loved Sandy. He would sit on her lap and purr like this was how it was meant to be from the beginning. Sammy loved me too. He would often join me on my desk while I worked. But Sammy chose Stephen, our younger son, as his person. Whenever Stephen was in the house, the two were inseparable.

Sammy lived with us for seventeen years until he, too, crossed the rainbow bridge. Our only consolation was that Casey (along with Sherlock, the dog from whom Casey inherited our love when he crossed the rainbow bridge at seventeen) was there to welcome him and lead him to wherever they would wait until their respective boys joined them in that place of bliss."

Lloyd isn't alone in his experience of an animal in need suddenly crossing his path and his feeling that the whole situation was helped along by a pet from across the rainbow bridge. Marian D. shares a very similar story:

"Lizzie Cat was my furry soul mate. I've had cats my whole life, but Lizzie was the kind of companion you get once in a lifetime. She was just special. When she passed away, I wasn't sure if I'd be able to love another cat. You always say that when you lose a pet, but this time, it really felt true. I was ready for her to be my last rescue.

Lizzie had other plans, apparently. The day after she passed, Samson showed up at the door. He was a gorgeous Ragdoll cat who had seen better days, and he was pretty wary of me. I thought, 'He must have been neglected and dumped.' And then I knew that Lizzie had sent him to me for help. After weeks of feeding him and patiently waiting for him to trust me, Samson decided that I was OK. Today, he is my spoiled, snuggly baby. Lizzie knew what she was doing."

"When [Lizzie] passed away, I wasn't sure if I'd be able to love another cat. . . . I was ready for her to be my last rescue. Lizzie had other plans."

Jennifer C. was led to a new kitty companion and healing from grief as well:

"When I was in my early twenties, my parents called to tell me that our family cat, Midnight, had passed. We had loved him for twenty years, from the day we found the tiny black puffball stranded and meowing loudly in our garage. Midnight was my closest companion growing up. He slept with me every night, snuggled me when I was sick, and made me smile every day.

A few days after he passed, I found myself at the local animal shelter with a coworker who had suddenly decided she wanted to spend her lunchbreak playing with kittens. She didn't know about Midnight. I was enjoying the break, sitting on the floor in the cat room with a mischievous orange kitten climbing on my shoulders. But I suddenly felt like something was pulling me to my left. There, sat a gangly older tabby kitten gently sniffing my purse. He looked up at me with big owl eyes, shy but not scared. He almost looked to be saying, 'I didn't want to bother you, but I'd appreciate some pets.'

Thirteen years later, that awkward little boy is my beautiful (and still incredibly polite) furry soulmate. He sleeps with me every night, snuggles me when I'm sick, and makes me smile every day. And I'm 100 percent sure my Midnight helped us find each other."

We've all been there, in the middle of events that somehow feel meant to happen. It's as if an unseen hand triggered a divine Rube Goldberg machine— everything is lining up and in motion. You no longer have control, but something mysterious and often beautiful is happening. We may try to chalk up these unexplainable occurrences as coincidences, events that happen at the same time by accident but seem to have some connection. But are they truly something greater, orchestrated by a greater power exactly as they were meant to be? In the case of pets no longer with us on earth, these events serve as a reminder of how much our loved ones are reaching out and communicating with us to give us care and even guidance. They know when we need another animal in our immediate lives.

"Thirteen years later,
that awkward little boy
is my beautiful (and still
incredibly polite) furry
soulmate.... And I'm
100 percent sure my
Midnight helped us
find each other."

Ladybugs

LUCK • PROTECTION • PROSPERITY • FULLNESS

You've probably made a wish on a ladybug at some point in your life. We welcome them when they come near and see them as wish granters if they land on us. Ladybugs have long been seen as a tiny symbol of big luck. Although thousands of varieties of ladybugs exist, some believe the brighter the red coat, the stronger the luck.

Although many legends surround the bugs, probably the most well-known is associated with the Virgin Mary coming to the rescue of farmers in desperate need during the Middle Ages. When pests threatened their crops, the farmers prayed to the Blessed Lady, the Virgin Mary, to deliver them and their lands. Suddenly, beneficial ladybugs appeared and saved the day. The farmers called them "our lady's birds," or lady beetles, which then became ladybugs.

Ladybugs are associated with strength and protection in their natural habitat as well. Although their delicate structure and bright colors make them pretty to observe, they have a subtle inner strength that helps them keep predators away. The little bugs leave foul-smelling yellow stains on surfaces when they're threatened. They are symbols of environmental security and prosperity even though they live for only a year. That fact can be a reminder to live our lives to the fullest. Many cultures see ladybugs as powerfully healing—for both the body and spirit. They are often associated with new happiness on the way.

Bethany Z. witnessed a ladybug bringing a renewed sense of happiness and healing into her life and the life of her dog after their companion passed away:

> "When I was growing up, my family had two yellow Labs: Lady and Molly. Lady was a few years older, but she was like a puppy again when

Molly came along. The two romped and played and snuffed at each other constantly. And when they were done, they curled up together for a nap. They were best friends.

When Lady died, Molly just wasn't herself. She moped around the house and seemed disinterested on walks. We understood that she was mourning her friend. A couple of weeks went by, and I was taking Molly for our usual walk. Suddenly, I just had a feeling like I should take a different route. We ended up passing a grassy field, and Molly started tugging hard on her leash. Happy to see her interested in something, I decided to let her run around. (She was used to playing off leash.)

Molly ran into the middle of the field and started jumping, rolling around, and doing that 'puppy pose' thing dogs do when they play together. I just stood there, watching in amazement. Then she came running back to me, looking like she had something wonderful to tell me. It was like she was saying, 'Did you see her, too?' And there, right on Molly's nose, was a ladybug. From that day on, Molly was back to her old self. It's like she knew her friend was there whenever she needed her."

Just as our pet companions may land in our lives unexpectedly and leave us too soon, ladybugs remind us to take in the beauty of living and the luck that surrounds us each day. Although we sometimes can't see how tiny moments can be powerful, ladybugs remind us that subtle is special too and that healing will come in small ways, in time.

Light Formations

PRESENCE · HOPE · PEACE

WHEN WE'RE MAKING THE DECISION TO END A PET'S SUFFERING OR GRIEVING A PET'S LOSS AFTER THE DECISION HAS BEEN MADE, IT'S EASY TO FEEL SURROUNDED BY DARKNESS AND CONFUSION. Questions of "why" and "what if" swirl in our heads and hearts. Is it really time to say good-bye? Will our days even feel the same? Will we connect with our pets again? Many pet owners experience symbols of light that help cut through the darkness and bring them reassuring "yes" answers that fill them with a certain peace for the present and hope to connect with their pets in a new way later.

These light formations may appear as anything from bright light seen with the naked eye shining on a spot where a pet loved to spend time, to orbs (balls of light or light energy) that inexplicably appear in a photo. But greater than what we see is the sense of comfort or hope the light can bring.

Lindsay S. believes that light was a message to let her know that she was making the right decision to let her senior dog find everlasting freedom:

"Many people adopt puppies or younger dogs, but older dogs may struggle to find their way out of a shelter to their forever home. I learned this hard truth when I started working for a rescue devoted to senior dogs. Instantly, Yeti grabbed my heart. He was this grumpy old man of a dog who liked his dinner on time and enjoyed a postmeal nap. In fact, his nicknames at the shelter were Sausage Monster and Saus Boss. While food was his favorite thing in the world, he hated the outdoors. How could I convince my adventure-seeking husband, Chris, who lives to hike, bike, and climb that this dog was meant for us?

Chris gave in, wondering if I had lost my mind. For the first few weeks with Yeti, I was worried about what I got us into, but soon all of his (what others might call) "bad behaviors" became endearing and funny. And you know the end of the story . . . Yeti won over Chris (and everyone else he met) with his ornery disposition. We loved to see him chase our other old grumpy pet and get excited about food, and we laughed at his absolute hatred of nature. Yeti declined mentally and physically faster than we expected, which made us both sad, but I couldn't imagine our time without him.

When it came time to say good-bye, we held Yeti in our laps and told him we loved him. It's the hardest decision a pet parent has to make, but when it's time, you know it's the right thing to do. Looking back now, I recall a few days before we said our good-byes that a circle of light that resembled a paw print appeared on the kitchen wall just above Yeti's food bowl. Just a reflection? I'd never noticed it before in the year that Yeti was part of our household. I like to see it as a sign of the peace we were able to give Yeti in that year and the more enduring peace he was ready to experience. Not today but someday when we're ready, we'll be able to make sure another senior dog feels loved."

Joanna C. felt peace and heart healing through a gift of light as well:

> "Sandy was the first dog that my husband and I adopted together, our sweet little fawn Chiweenie girl. We loved everything about her, from her stylish white socks and very pink nose to her joyful dancing at breakfast and snuggles at bedtime. Sandy was our baby. She had the run of the house and a designated spot on our bed, which she slept on every night.
>
> After the birth of our son, we realized that we had outgrown our house. We found a big, beautiful Cape Cod, not too far away, with a yard that we just knew Sandy was going to love. Sadly, she passed away unexpectedly before she ever got to see it. We moved into our dream home a few weeks later, but it didn't feel as dreamy without our girl.
>
> I was heartbroken at having to leave the place where Sandy had spent her nine years loving us, like I was leaving her behind. But, when I took photos of our unpacked home to send to a friend, I discovered that Sandy was with me all along. I had taken three different pictures of my bedroom from different angles. In each one, a glowing white orb hung over Sandy's spot on the bed. I knew it was her. And now I know that the ones who love us are always with us. I'm so thankful to Sandy for giving me that."

We can always look to the light as a reminder of the brightness loved ones bring to our lives. The best news: True light never fades. We stayed connected through an eternal presence and the assurance that we will be reunited in heaven someday.

"When I took photos of our unpacked home to send to a friend . . . a glowing white orb hung over Sandy's spot on the bed. . . . The ones who love us are always with us."

Movements/
Moving Objects

PRESENCE · COMFORT · CONNECTION · POSSIBILITY

FROM SCURRYING KITTENS AND PUPPIES UNDER OUR FEET TO OLDER PETS WHO MAY LUMBER DOWN STAIRS OR WELCOME A HOIST ONTO COUCHES OR HUMAN BEDS, WE GET ACCUSTOMED TO THE CONSTANT MOVEMENTS OF PETS THROUGHOUT OUR LIVES. The house can seem so deafeningly quiet and absolutely still after a pet crosses the rainbow bridge. How do we discover a healthy rhythm of life again?

Don't be surprised if your pets appear in those moments! Our companions seem to know when we need a reminder of the fullness of and possibility in each day and that their love lives on with us.

"The craziest thing happened: the door swung open. We both saw it, but neither one of us can explain it, except to say that Moe missed us as much as we missed him."

Todd L. continues to feel his dog, Moe, move throughout his life. Here is one time he experienced Moe's presence strongly:

"My wife and I had this Great Pyrenees mix named Moe—just a fluffy, white, gentle giant of a dog. He really was the best boy. He never misbehaved, never needed to hear the word 'no.' All you had to do was give him a look or a nod and he knew what you wanted from him. But he also knew how to get what *he* wanted.

Moe's bed was on the first floor in the living room. Every night, we'd say good night and he would go to his bed. And every night, Moe would wait until we turned out our lights, then tiptoe up the stairs, push the bedroom door open with his nose, and jump up into the bed with us so softly that it was like he was hoping we wouldn't notice. He just loved being around us. We had no idea how much we'd miss that until he was gone.

A few weeks after we had to say good-bye, Moe stopped by. We had just turned out the lights to go to bed, and I was midsentence when my wife shushed me and told me to listen. I swore I could hear Moe's toenails on the wood floors. Then the craziest thing happened: the door swung open. We both saw it, but neither one of us can explain it, except to say that Moe missed us as much as we missed him."

Rebecca B. has experienced the power of movement as communication from her dog as well:

"Jonah took his first breath in my hands, as I gently cuddled him straight from his mother's belly. As a veterinarian technician with no children, I took him in as my child—later to find out he was deaf. Jonah came to work with me every day, and everyone loved his happy personality.

Jonah eventually gained human brothers to watch over. We were always together. He assisted me in rehabilitating wildlife orphans and seemed to enjoy every moment as I did. Life was good. Life was simple. Life was precious.

When Jonah's body grew old, I did whatever I could to help him along—even sleeping on the couch for a year so I could be near him and listen to him breathe. Feeling his soft fur while I closed my eyes relaxed me. But the day I knew would come was closing in on us. Sadness overwhelmed me, knowing the heartache that was approaching. Jonah took his last breath in my arms on my kitchen floor and the world stopped. Everything stood still and there was silence. My first baby was gone. My heart was crushed.

For months after Jonah's death, the kitchen table would move about a foot sideways. Every night. I knew it was him. Jonah would lay against it to get cool on the tile floor at night. My heart still yearns for him."

Although nothing can completely erase the pain of losing a beloved companion, it's comforting to know that in some way, the door to the connection with our pets remains open even after they leave this earthly life. We ourselves can stay open to the lessons they've shared with us in the past and the blessings that their memories continue to bring to us. Those reminders of the love possible in this world (and beyond) are what can truly move us toward healing.

"Jonah took his first breath in my hands. . . . Jonah took his last breath in my arms. . . . For months after Jonah's death, the kitchen table would move about a foot sideways. Every night. I knew it was him."

Noseprints

HUMOR • CURIOSITY • APPRECIATION FOR LIFE

It's human to overcomplicate things. Pets can teach us to appreciate the little things and simply run with whatever the day gives us—whether it's a piece of fuzz or a bright, new squeaky tennis ball. Animals can be our therapists with fur, feathers, or fins. So, what happens when they leave earth and we struggle to feel the loving licks and laughter at their antics?

Just watch and see what small messages appear to help us remember how to wonder again. If our beloved pets have left their imprints on our heart, it's not surprising that they might leave us noseprint messages to prompt a smile.

When Josh L. brought himself to clean the family's sliding glass door after his dog, Brick, passed, something surprising happened:

> "Our pittie rescue, Brick, looked like a beast but was as silly and sweet as they come. He'd scramble up the couch and lay all sixty pounds of his muscular body across you with a big harrumph. Then he'd whine and wiggle and lick your face until you rubbed his belly. When he wanted to go out, he'd sit at the sliding glass door with his snout fully pressed up against it and blow raspberries. You just couldn't be unhappy around him. We were constantly laughing—and wiping noseprints and slobber off the door.
>
> When we had to put him down, the house was just so quiet and sad without him. Eventually, we tidied up his toys and put away his bowls. But we couldn't bring ourselves to clean the glass for some time. Looking at the noseprints made us smile, and we needed that. Finally, we said a tearful good-bye to Brick and wiped the glass clean.
>
> The next morning, we woke to find noseprints and smudges on the glass. My wife and I looked at each other, wide-eyed and wondering whether we'd both dreamed that we'd cleaned the glass. Then we burst out laughing. It was just Brick doing what he always did—putting a smile on our faces."

Finding a noseprint is often a message to get out of your head and into your heart, to live life in a hands-on, noseprint-leaving sort of way again. Be curious. Have an adventure. Follow your senses. But most of all, do things that make you smile and laugh and feel the richness of life's experiences.

"Finally, we wiped the glass clean. The next morning, we woke to find noseprints. . . . It was just Brick doing what he always did—putting a smile on our faces."

Other Animals

COMFORT • AFFIRMATION • INSIGHT

ANIMALS HAVE THEIR OWN UNIQUE WAY OF COMMUNICATING WITH HUMANS AND WITH EACH OTHER. Many pet owners say they have felt their pet communicate to them through another animal after they have crossed the rainbow bridge. Watch for these special animal messengers to show up in your life after the loss of a pet. They most often bring messages of comfort that your pet is at peace beyond this world and that you will be OK after a time of grieving as well.

Chris P. has no doubt that his cat sent him comfort through another animal:

> "The day after my cat, Greta, passed, I noticed another cat at my sliding glass door. I had never seen this cat before, and when I went to open the door, she scurried away. I haven't seen her since. That was a sign to tell me that Greta was OK."

Vandana B. has also felt the love and comfort of her most special dog from beyond the rainbow bridge through other animals popping into her life:

"I've had pets (cats and dogs) since the day I came into this world, and I remember the names of all my furry babies since I was age five. I see them and feel them in my dreams. My special baby was a Doberman rescue pup named Cezar. When I adopted him, Cezar was barely six months old but was fighting a severe gastrointestinal infection. He was on the verge of death. I nursed him day and night, and in turn he gave his 100 percent love and loyalty. He became my protector.

At the time, I was in a bad marriage—with physical, mental, and emotional abuse. My only support was my baby Cezar. He used to come in between my ex and me when my ex was about to hit me. Cezar took so many such hits for me, I cannot count. And one day while saving me, he gave his life.

He is forever in my heart. I still feel guilty. But whenever I call him while I'm hiking, out of nowhere a dog appears and licks me. I've experienced that so many times. I take it as a sign that my Cezar is telling me that he is OK with God at the rainbow bridge, and he is still with me.

Right now, I have three kitty boys, all rescued. I know in my heart that my life is better because of all these furry babies who help me to heal and cope with my pain. I wait for that day when I'll meet all my furry babies who are waiting for me. I owe them my life."

"Whenever I call [Cezar] while I'm hiking, out of nowhere a dog appears and licks me. . . . My Cezar is telling me that he is OK with God at the rainbow bridge, and he is still with me."

Sometimes a pet's communications also nudge you toward a certain choice or path in your life. Sara W. welcomed a nudge toward more grateful living from one pet rat through another:

> "My fancy rat, Gus Grissom, passed rather unexpectedly. He was my 'heart rat'—what rat owners often call the rat with which they connect and bond the most. Because rats have such short life spans, it's common to have many over the years. But some just touch you in a special way more than others. Gus was cuddly and loving but at the same time mischievous and fun. The last night I spent with him, he was trying to steal the mint leaves out of my mojito one minute and seeking snuggles the next. That was Gus!
>
> After he passed away, I felt a sudden urge to dedicate time each morning to snuggles with his brother, Buzz Aldrin. (Yes, all of my rats have been named after US astronauts.) Through physical closeness with Buzz, I could still feel a piece of Gus. I've often thought that maybe that nudge toward a new morning routine came from Gus.
>
> Caring for fancy rats has given me a whole new perspective. They live with such zest in their short lives! Every day for them and with them is a gift."

Our pets know us and read us well—often, better than we read ourselves. We benefit greatly by paying attention to the ways they reach out to us.

"Through physical closeness with Buzz, I could still feel a piece of Gus. I've often thought that maybe that nudge toward a new morning routine came from Gus."

Paw Prints

PROTECTION • COMPANIONSHIP • STRENGTH

THOSE FAMILIAR PAWS, WHETHER TINY OR BROAD, ARE ETCHED INTO OUR MEMORIES. The sound of them scratching at the door to be let in or out, or trotting across the floor to greet us or entice us to play. The feel of them pressing into our laps or legs as a reminder of their presence and love. The telltale marks we see across the just-mopped floor or tramping through the garden. We try not to laugh as we scold the trespassing.

The paw prints of beloved pets leave imprints on our hearts that don't easily fade. In fact, some pet owners continue to see physical prints that let them know their companion is still with them and watching over them.

Krista W. couldn't believe her eyes when her daughter called for her to come and see how their cat had come for a visit:

> "Nellie was a sometimes-sweet, sometimes-sassy petite girl. She didn't like everyone, but she loved my daughter, Olivia. Nellie was constantly wrapping herself around Liv's legs and pressing her tiny paws into her bare feet, making Liv giggle. When Liv didn't feel well, Nellie curled up in bed with her. And anytime Liv sat and 'read' in the nook under her bedroom window, Nellie would be her captive audience. They were inseparable.
>
> My daughter was six when Nellie passed away, and she was completely heartbroken. I told her what parents tell their kids—that Nellie was still watching over her, even if she couldn't see her. Well, one day, Nellie proved me right. Liv came running into the kitchen, excitedly bouncing up and down while telling me, 'Nellie was here!'
>
> I thought Liv was imagining it or making it up, like little kids do.

"There were tiny paw prints in the fabric that hadn't been there before. . . . Nellie really was watching over our little girl."

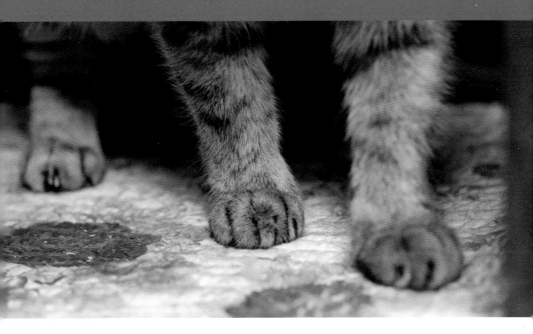

But she dragged me by the hand over to her little reading nook, and sure enough, there were tiny paw prints in the fabric that hadn't been there before. I racked my brain, trying to figure out how she could have made them. I covertly looked at her stuffed animals to see if any had realistic paws while saying, 'I see!' But I finally had to accept that those paw prints were just too real. Nellie really was watching over our little girl."

When we've walked so many steps and days together, we fall in sync with our pets. They want us to know that kind of love and loyalty never ends. Our pets are still by our side and waiting to walk with us to new places someday. We need not be afraid of what comes next when we feel the peace our pets are experiencing now.

Rainbows

PROMISE • REUNION • PEACE • BLESSING

IT'S NOT UNCOMMON FOR US TO TALK ABOUT OUR PRECIOUS PETS CROSSING THE RAINBOW BRIDGE WHEN THEY PASS FROM THIS EARTHLY WORLD. The term came about from a poem of the same name. Although the exact origin of the poem is disputed, most pet owners won't dispute the peace it brings them in a time of loss. Its words have been widely shared on everything from bookmarks and prints to blankets and candles. The message is that we can look to the rainbow bridge, an overpass that connects heaven and earth. Here, we discover a promised place where we can reunite for eternity with our departed furry friends. How comforting to know it's just a matter of time until we are with them again in a place of joy!

The connection of rainbows to hope is nothing new. God shares a rainbow as a blessing and promise to Noah after the great flood. When we see a rainbow, we are reassured that one day everything will be restored and beautiful again in the way God intended. It's a sign of a new beginning to come. We can be comforted by the thought of our pets enjoying that beauty now, waiting for us to join them.

The feelings that seeing a rainbow can bring are particularly special to me:

> During my fourteen-plus years with my rescue dog, Bella, by my side, we saw several rainbows together. The first time it happened, I was brought to tears in a very meaningful way, realizing the immensity of the gift of Bella. Bella had been instrumental in my healing from addiction and in coming to faith in God. The beauty of the moment and our lives woven together struck me.
>
> Bella passed at around sixteen years of age, but the blessings we shared live on. When I was on my way to pick up her ashes from the vet, I saw a

low-lying rainbow, which happened to be a double one! It reminded me of all the times we experienced the beauty of rainbows together and gave me an overwhelming sense that everything is and will be OK. It was comfort and a promise. I am comforted all over again whenever I see a rainbow.

If you see a rainbow at just the right time, it may be a reminder that what we can physically see and hold on earth is fleeting but still a beautiful blessing that remains with us in our hearts. Even once it has faded from view, close your eyes and see that rainbow. See that beloved animal companion. Sense that something good and hopeful is around the next corner. Know that we will all be reunited in a beautiful place someday.

"It reminded me of all the times we experienced the beauty of rainbows together and gave me an overwhelming sense that everything is and will be OK."

Robins

HOPE · REBIRTH · RENEWAL

IN CERTAIN REGIONS, THE EMERGENCE OF RED-BREASTED ROBINS AFTER A LONG WINTER IS A VERY WELCOME SIGN. Spring, with all of its accompanying hope and new growth, has arrived! Spotting a robin after the death of a loved one can bring the same sense of promise and renewal. Even after a dark, cold time, the light and joy of spring arrive again. We need only patience and wisdom to see that the next season (of the year and of life) is right around the corner. In that way, a robin is a sign of rebirth from those we miss, reminding us that they are now beautiful and whole in their new season, new life beyond earth. That's a comfort.

Birds can also carry a message for how we live our lives now. We can learn from the energy of birds. They have a certain way of being that encourages us to face tough seasons and unexpected turns with optimism and a song in our hearts. We need not worry or feel burdened. We will feel the sun shining on our faces again when we're ready to move forward with determination.

Although her canine companion passed away some time ago, Kelly T. continues to find joy and peace at the sight of a robin:

"Toby taught me to find joy in all the little things. . . . To this day, every time I see the first robin in spring, I think of him and the gifts of happiness, love, and friendship he gave me."

"I had been going through a rough time at school when my family surprised me with Toby, a happy, hyper shepherd mix they found at our local shelter. It's pretty hard to be upset around a puppy—especially one that won't stop licking your face.

Being outside with Toby, for whom everything was new and amazing, helped me get out of my funk and start noticing the good things. And just a few weeks later, it was spring. There were new flowers to smell and new birds to chase. (Toby especially loved the robins, which were always at puppy level, picking around in the grass.)

Toby taught me to find joy in all the little things. He crossed the rainbow bridge a long time ago now, but I've kept that lesson close to me ever since. To this day, every time I see the first robin in spring, I think of him and the gifts of happiness, love, and friendship he gave me."

Consider the birds. They appear as symbols of hope and strength throughout ancient texts, including the Bible. And they continue to appear to us today to share spiritual messages. Robins bring such a sense of peace and closeness with those who have passed that they are sometimes called remembrance robins. Allow them to help you remember all the experiences you shared with your beloved pet, but also to see a new season in life that is ready for you to enter and discover beauty.

Storms/Weather

RELEASE • RELIEF • CLEANSING

IF WE PAY ATTENTION, WEATHER CAN REALLY SPEAK TO US AT JUST THE RIGHT MOMENT. And we often need to look beyond just the sunny skies and bright rainbows. Power and meaning can come through even in those moments that look dark and sometimes scary. In fact, the way we see things can turn a storm into a blessing. No matter your spiritual beliefs, consider the truth in this quote from Mother Sha-Riah, a shaman: "The wind howls, and rips through the atmosphere, you can almost see the air. It clears and cleans the atmosphere leaving behind a freshness that is a delight to breathe in, and there is a sense of freedom in each breath."

Storms can bring a sense of relief—especially in a time of hurt and grieving. There's that sudden howling and disruption of everyday life, but then that sense of cleansing and pressure relieved from the air. It's a natural, even beautiful, process when you can look at it objectively. Can you feel it as it's described? Have you ever felt that in a time of loss?

Richard K. shares his stormy experience when his dog buddy, Luke, passed on:

> "It was summertime, and Luke wasn't doing so well. We had an appointment set for 5:00 p.m. for the vet to come and help him pass. By midmorning I knew he couldn't hold out until 5:00. I was able to get a mobile vet to come to the house earlier and help him along.
>
> Usually in the summertime where I live, you can hear constant sounds from an airport not too far away, landscapers and contractors, and people going about their day in the neighborhood. At the time Luke passed, it was like a plastic bubble over our house. It was so silent. None of those 'normal' sounds were present.
>
> Then at 5:00, right around the time the other vet would have come, a thunderstorm seemed to come out of nowhere. Luke was letting me know it was OK. He was telling me that I made the right choice for not waiting, like a thank-you."

See the message and take courage in a storm. If you haven't yet fully grieved, the arrival of a storm at a certain moment may be giving you permission to howl. If you're struggling to see purpose, be open to the cleansing of a storm and see it as a chance for a fresh start and new growth in your life. If you're wondering whether you made the right decision at the right time, feel the power of nature's timing and trust that cleansing came also for your beloved companion.

"At the time Luke passed, it was like a plastic bubble over our house. It was so silent. . . . Then, a thunderstorm seemed to come out of nowhere. Luke was letting me know it was OK."

Watch for equally meaningful but gentler changes in weather as well, especially if your pet was an extremely sensitive and gentle soul versus a bundle of boundless energy. Just as the ways in which we communicate as people are different, so, too, are pets' ways of communicating—even after they've crossed the rainbow bridge. Lee Ann K. felt a bond with her dog through a sentimentally located and sudden breeze on an otherwise still day:

> "I had my first Golden Retriever for thirteen years. Over those years we were inseparable. I taught Lady how to swim and enjoy the water when she was only ten weeks old. I taught her to stop at every corner and not move until I said it was safe to go when we took our walks. I taught her how to roll over, how to play hide and seek, how to sit when someone came to pet her.
>
> Lady would follow me everywhere and would lick my hand and thank me for being a friend. She could run like the wind and make me laugh at her silly antics. Her bed was next to mine at night, so every morning she would come and stare at me until I opened my eyes. When I gave in, her tail would wag like she hadn't seen me in years!
>
> I loved that dog and never realized how much she taught me until she was gone. Mutual respect, patience, and unconditional dedication. Dogs speak with their eyes; we had many silent conversations, my Lady dog and I, but they all ended with a mutual love we shared for one another.
>
> On her passing, my son and daughter-in-law gave me a dogwood tree to plant her ashes under in the yard. I see it every day from my kitchen window. I had a very hard time letting her go and would cry thinking about her. One year to the day after we buried her, I was standing next to the tree. It was a warm, still morning. I talked to her as if she was still here. A beautiful breeze came up and brushed my face and left as quickly as it came. I felt her tongue lick my hand. I really loved that dog."

"A beautiful breeze came up
and brushed my face and left
as quickly as it came. I felt
[Lady's] tongue lick my hand."

Sunbeams

CALM • REST • REFOCUS • WONDER

HAVE YOU EVER STOPPED TO MARVEL AT THE SUN AND HOW ITS RAYS CAN FEEL LIKE BEAMS OF HOPE ENTERING OUR WORLD? If not, you're missing out! Just like the pets who have been part of our families, the sun brings a sense of warmth into our lives. Sunbeams can also bring wonder and inspiration as we go about our day and find them crossing our path, especially at a time we may be feeling rushed or in a dark place. Suddenly, our focus is drawn to the light and away from whatever we thought was a life-or-death matter (but totally wasn't) just a few minutes earlier.

Taking in the light with our eyes and absorbing the warmth all over our body can give us that "everything is going to be OK" feeling—almost like watching the spark in a pet's eyes or stroking the fur of a special companion. Our blood pressure calms and the stress response slows.

"Suddenly, I could see [Percy]. It was just for a moment, but it was like the sunshine was looking for *him*. It gave me hope that he'll always feel that warmth on his soft bunny fur."

Chris M. shares a sunbeam experience that warmed his soul:

"I lost my sweet little Holland Lop, Percy, just a few months ago. For such a small bunny, he had a big personality. Percy was not only a spoiled little prince, he was also a tiny Houdini. You just couldn't keep him in an enclosure if he didn't want to be there. And he rarely wanted to be there.

Whenever Percy would escape, it was always in search of sunshine. He loved nothing more than falling asleep in the warmth of the afternoon sun. In fact, it's what he was doing when he passed away.

I was sitting on the couch a few days later when a sunbeam broke through the clouds and fell onto the living room floor. And suddenly, like dust in the sunlight, I could see him. It was just for a moment, but it was like the sunshine was looking for *him*. It gave me hope that, wherever he is, he'll always feel that warmth on his soft bunny fur."

Jennifer L. also relishes a sunbeam experience, related to her cats:

> "Having cats as part of our family was always a reminder to me to slow down and savor the being (not doing) in life. Even now, when I see sunbeams dance across a room in my home, I can still picture my sister and brother cats, Bonnie and Clyde, searching for the biggest sliver of sunlight and warmth and nestling into the spot, all snuggled together. Sometimes, when I'm feeling particularly crazed with the busyness of life, I feel like God directs my attention to the sunbeams with a gentle message from Bonnie and Clyde."

You, too, may discover sunbeams in a place your pet enjoyed lounging as a reminder to find rest in this often-crazy life and hurried world. Don't ignore the message—our pets often sense just what we need, in this world and beyond. Listening to their signs can bring us rest and comfort.

"Sometimes, when I'm feeling particularly crazed with the busyness of life, I feel like God directs my attention to the sunbeams with a gentle message from Bonnie and Clyde."

Tags Jangling

JOY • ENERGY • CURIOSITY

THAT JINGLING, JANGLING OF PET TAGS IS AN INSTANTLY RECOG-
NIZABLE SOUND WHEN ANIMALS ARE PART OF YOUR FAMILY. It's a
kind of music for a pet lover's soul. The noise often accompanies running and
frolicking and just generally joyful play and activity. Then when a pet crosses
the rainbow bridge, your house and yard may suddenly seem way too quiet.
The thoughts in your head seem too noisy, and you miss the cheerful clinking
of your pet's comings and goings.

But if you listen carefully, you may hear those tags as clear as wind chimes
again. It's a soft song your pet is sending you to give you peace and permission
to jump back into life again.

At first, Deanna P. and her husband couldn't believe their ears when they heard
their dog's tags:

> "We adopted Disco from a rescue in Arkansas. The family who had him
> couldn't manage his endless hunting dog energy. My husband and I had
> wide-open fields all around us, so we were able to give Disco the space to
> roam and run. In return, he gave us unconditional love and tons of enter-
> tainment. When we let him out in the morning, we'd hear his tags jangling
> endlessly as he raced around trying to catch every bird and critter he could
> see. Even when his arthritis got bad, he found the strength to give them all
> a good chase. It was his thrill in life, and it gave us joy to watch him run.
>
> My husband went away on business when Disco was very old and
> weak. It was that weekend when Disco passed away. I didn't want to
> upset my husband while he was far from home, but as soon as he came
> through the front door, I broke down crying and shared the sad news.

"Some sort of peace came over me, even then, in my grief, knowing that our beloved dog wasn't truly lost to us. We would hear his tags again, about a decade later when we moved out of our home."

My husband seemed more bewildered than upset. 'But I just heard him,' he said. 'When I was coming up the walkways. His tags were jangling like crazy from back in the tall grass.' Some sort of peace came over me, even then, in my grief, knowing that our beloved dog wasn't truly lost to us. We would hear his tags again, about a decade later when we moved out of our home. I knew he was chasing after us, and I was glad knowing that he wouldn't ever stop."

It's easy to get stuck in our grief when our pets pass. All the family and friends in the world may try to comfort us and let us know it's OK to heal with time. But the clearest message may come from your pet—sharing their current peace and reminding you not to close yourself off from all the life and beauty in your days still waiting to be discovered.

Touches

COMFORT • LOVE • HEALING

I<small>T'S AMAZING BUT MAYBE NOT SURPRISING</small>: P<small>ET OWNERS HAVE</small> <small>BEEN FOUND TO HAVE LOWER BLOOD PRESSURE</small>, lower triglyceride and cholesterol levels, lower risk of depression, and fewer visits to doctors than those without pets in their lives. The companionship is healing but so is the power of touch. Petting or holding an animal can be incredibly therapeutic.

But how do we hold on to that feeling and comfort when we lose our animal friend and healer? It may not be as difficult as you might think.

Jillian R. didn't quite realize the strength of her bond with her cat until she felt what she had thought was physically impossible:

> "I know it's weird to say that a cat is your rock, but my tabby cat, Penelope, was my rock. I struggle with depression, and she was always right by my side. She did this one thing whenever I would lie down: She'd find my hand and press her little face into it. She'd keep doing it until I started actively petting her. Then she would stand on my chest and push her face right into mine. Just that little bit of love was a huge help.
>
> When she died, I was heartbroken. I curled up on my bed, unable to cry or move or sleep. And then I felt it—her little face pressing into my hand. I could feel her whiskers and the soft fur on her cheek. Afraid the feeling would disappear, I just stayed completely still. But she kept nudging and pressing. When I finally lifted my hand to pet her, I felt her two little paws on my chest and the light brush of her nose on my cheek. And then she was gone. I think it was Penelope's way of letting me know she was still there for me."

"Penelope was my rock. . . . When she died,
I was heartbroken. I curled up on my bed,
unable to cry or move or sleep. And then I
felt it—her little face pressing into my hand."

If you feel your pet through physical touch, appreciate the sensory gift you've been given. Take in the comfort and the peace that pass through the experience. Then also use the communication as an impetus to find more ways to fulfill your need for touch—you can try everything from simple hugs and hand-holding with those you love to massage and laying on of hands. Touch is our first sensation and can be powerfully healing and capable of communicating love.

Vocalizations

STRENGTH · FAITH · COURAGE

♫

Signs from our pets in heaven can be as subtle as wispy clouds or soft feathers and as majestic as soaring eagles or bright rainbows. But they're not always silent. Sometimes, they are loud and clear . . . and quite familiar. We may doubt what we hear at first, but a pet's recognizable voice is difficult to brush off. Maybe that's what it takes for us to listen to a message our pet is trying to send.

Pet owners who hear their beloved pet's meow, chirp, yip, bark, squeak, or other vocalization are likely in need of a very direct sign from their pet in a time of struggling faith or hope. Gentler signs may be missed, but the message of daily strength and encouragement will come through more clearly in a pet's voice if we're open to listening and believing.

"I thought I was going crazy when I heard it. . . .
Then, a few weeks and a few conversations later,
a friend of mine heard him too. . . . From then
on, I just stopped and appreciated whenever
Gus dropped by to say hello."

Liza L. got past her initial disbelief to accept and enjoy her interactions with her cat, Gus:

"My baby Gus was a talker. He'd just have full conversations with anyone willing to chat. Sometimes he'd meow, sometimes he'd yowl, but mostly he'd chitter and trill like he was trying to form actual words. When he passed, I think I missed hearing his voice the most. That's why I thought I was going crazy when I heard it again.

I walked in the door after work, and I swear I heard him greet me like he used to. I shrugged it off as a long day, but I heard him again a couple of weeks later. Now I really thought I was losing it. Then, a few weeks and a few conversations later, a friend of mine heard him too. He stopped midsentence and looked like he was listening for something. Then he asked if I'd gotten another cat. When I said no, he said he was sure he heard Gus talking. That sealed it for me—I wasn't crazy. From then on, I just stopped and appreciated whenever Gus dropped by to say hello."

Grieving is a journey. It can help to have a strengthening soundtrack. Hear the hopeful voice and perspective a pet may be trying to share, letting you know they are at peace. Listen for encouragement in the music of nature and everyday life. Be open to the messages of love and support those around you want to share.

Warmth

LOVE • COMFORT • PRESENCE

When movies or TV shows portray characters receiving messages from beyond this world, the communications often seem to come with a sudden influx of cold air. But if you dig into actual spiritual moments people describe, you may be more likely to find an experience of sudden warmth—whether a feeling of heartwarming inside or a space in the environment feeling warmer.

Our time with pets is also associated with warmth—both physical as we stroke and snuggle with furry companions and emotional as we form bonds of love and companionship. What a blessing to continue feeling warmth through our pets even after they have left this life!

Kim M. shares how her grandmother felt a sense of warmth in her dog's favorite sofa spot after Buffy crossed the rainbow bridge:

> "Before my grandfather passed, he convinced my grandmother to get a Jack Russell. They had always had bigger, more mellow dogs. But for some reason, he wanted this little dog. They got Buffy straight from a breeder, who swore she was purebred. But Buffy never really filled out her Jack Russell genes. For one thing, she was tiny. For another, her ears stood straight up where they were supposed to flop. She was just an odd creature, and way more energetic than either of them had bargained for.
>
> Her high spirits turned out to be a blessing after my grandfather passed shortly thereafter. She kept my grandmother company for fourteen years, but she also kept her on her toes. In the evening, after a day of walks and play, the two would snuggle up on the couch together to watch *Jeopardy!* and *Wheel of Fortune.*

"She took my hand and pressed it into the couch next to her. It was warm. Much warmer, in fact, than any other spot on the couch. My grandmother said that she could feel Buffy tucked against her leg."

A few weeks after Buffy crossed the rainbow bridge, I was sitting next to my grandmother while she watched her shows. Suddenly, she looked down at her hip. Then she touched a spot on the couch next to her and almost jumped. I asked her what was wrong and she said, 'Nothing. Buffy's here.' She took my hand and pressed it into the couch next to her. It was warm. Much warmer, in fact, than any other spot on the couch. My grandmother said that she could feel Buffy tucked against her leg, just like she used to be, and I believed her.

My grandmother seemed just a bit more relaxed after that night. I think having that experience gave her faith that Buffy and my grandfather were both waiting for her."

If you experience a feeling of sudden warmth in a pet's favorite place or unexplainably within your heart, take it in as a sign of love and comfort. Allow your pet to share a little bit of sunshine from heaven to bring peace into your day.

Water

CALM • CLEANSING • RENEWAL

GAZE UPON A BODY OF WATER AND YOU WILL FEEL YOUR BLOOD PRESSURE DROP. Soak in a warm bath and feel the weight of your worries lifted. Water has a strong association with calm that began quite some time ago. How our brain reacts to water goes way back to our ancestors and their quest for survival. When finding water on the move was key to life or death, the sight of a water source was incredibly calming. In fact, just the sight (or sound) of water could trigger a calming brain response—something we carry with us even today.

Water is also associated with new life and healing—common themes you'll find throughout the Bible. Modern science agrees that water is life, as our bodies are estimated to be made up of 60 to 70 percent water. It's no wonder that humans and animals alike are drawn to water. It speaks to us and offers a peace that's both tangible and spiritual.

Allison S. felt peace through the sight of water on the day she released her Lab to cross the rainbow bridge:

> "From the moment we brought our chocolate Lab girl home, Jemma was constantly trying to get into water. When I would try to water the garden, she would jump between me and the hose. If there was a puddle anywhere in the neighborhood, she would find it. I even found her plotting to join the kids' baths some nights. But Jemma's favorite way to get wet was to swim in the lake. Even if we started out in the canoe, she couldn't resist diving in. Her puppy energy seemed like it could go on forever!
>
> When Jemma suddenly became ill, we were heartbroken. The vets ran tests and tried all sorts of treatments for suspected diagnoses, but they couldn't figure out what was bringing her down and very quickly. All

that was clear was that our sweet girl was ready to be at peace.

On our way to the vet, we rode past the lake, Jemma's lake. The winds roared all around us that fall day, even shaking the car a bit. My husband was focused on driving, but my mind was wandering everywhere. Were we making the right decision? How would we go through our days without Jemma? Then I glanced over at the lake and saw that the water was miraculously calm. Trees were blowing, but the water was still. I could feel Jemma's slow breathing on the back seat next to me. It seemed like the first time in weeks she wasn't restless and agitated. I just had this sense that Jemma was already on her way to finding puddles and lakes across the rainbow bridge and our hearts would heal if we gave them some quiet space to seal memories of Jemma within."

When you have a pet who was a water lover in this life, the symbolism of the water may feel even stronger when that pet passes. But spending time around a body of water can help you move toward a sense of peace in knowing that you did all you could for your pet's well-being and knowing that true healing is at work for your pet and your soul.

your
Memories
& Signs
Journal

Help for the
Healing Process

THE MORE I SPOKE WITH PET LOVERS IN THE PROCESS OF WRITING THIS BOOK, THE MORE AMAZED I BECAME at the strength of the bonds we form with our pets. Those bonds aren't broken by physical separation in this world.

At first, when our loved ones leave us and transition on, we feel a huge void. We are left to find new routine in our lives. But as we grieve and move toward healing, it's comforting to remember that it is not "good-bye" but "until we meet again." Even though we grieve tremendously, as you've seen through the stories shared, we will see and feel signs from our loved ones that celebrate our special connection and bring comfort.

Our pets know how much we love them and want to let us know that they are at so much peace, whole and renewed in their new life. Although this time here without them will feel long, in reality we will meet them again in the blink of an eye. In the meantime, we do our best in this world to honor them, their signs, and their teachings. We strive to pass along their unconditional love that they so freely have given to us.

I hope and pray you have found some peace in these signs and words from those who have suffered and are still suffering from their losses but have found bright spots and eternal meaning in connections with their pets. I pray that you may find joy and peace knowing our pets are in a good place, and that they are still with us in our hearts.

It's OK to grieve. It's OK to feel all sorts of feelings. Writing about your special memories with your pet and the lessons learned through your pet is a path to receiving love and healing. For wherever you are on that journey, I've given you space to start or continue on pages 108–113. Try recording all the ways your pet has been a blessing in your life and how those blessings will remain with you— both in your heart and in tangible ways you can share with others.

At the same time, stay open to signs in the here and now. Ask, seek, and receive. Your loved one is waiting. Keeping a journal of these signs from heaven can help remind you of the peace there is to be found in this world and in the heaven beyond. You'll find space and helpful prompts to begin that practice on pages 114–124. It's a way to celebrate eternal bonds, find inspiration and guidance, and feel a higher sense of love and purpose.

BLESSINGS FROM PADDY

Fran H. shares how she learned the joy of riding horses from her beloved horse who has passed on, and how much her horse helped her through a very hard time:

"My beautiful Morgan horse—Brentwood Patriot, or 'Paddy' for short—and I had a truly close and rewarding relationship. I had wanted a horse as a child and my father would say 'someday.' Finally, when I was forty, my 'someday' came. I was able to start riding lessons and purchase seven-year-old Paddy.

We spent many happy hours together, whether trail riding or bonding while I groomed him. He also saw me through the loss of my beloved husband. Being at the barn where nothing had changed, when at home nothing was the same, was as necessary as eating and sleeping.

We would ride through the quiet woods where deer or turkey ran ahead or arrive on a ridge where you could see for miles and marvel at God's beautiful creation. It was there I could find peace and serenity.

I lost Paddy when he was twenty-eight. Although I still ride along with my twelve-year-old granddaughter, who is discovering the joy of horses that I learned from Paddy, I keep a special place in my heart for my 'someday' horse."

Lasting Memories
& Lessons

_____

_____

_____

_____

_____

_____

_____

_____

_____

_____

_____

_____

_____

_____

_____

_____

_____

_____

Signs from Heaven All Around

Date

_____

What I saw/heard/felt:

_____

_____

_____

What I sense it meant:

_____

_____

_____

How it made me feel:

_____

_____

_____

How I plan to act on the sign/message:

_____

_____

_____

Date

What I saw/heard/felt:

What I sense it meant:

How it made me feel:

How I plan to act on the sign/message:

Date

What I saw/heard/felt:

What I sense it meant:

How it made me feel:

How I plan to act on the sign/message:

Date

_____

What I saw/heard/felt:

_____

_____

_____

_____

What I sense it meant:

_____

_____

_____

_____

How it made me feel:

_____

_____

_____

_____

How I plan to act on the sign/message:

_____

_____

_____

_____

Date

What I saw/heard/felt:

What I sense it meant:

How it made me feel:

How I plan to act on the sign/message:

Date

_____

What I saw/heard/felt:

_____

_____

_____

_____

What I sense it meant:

_____

_____

_____

_____

How it made me feel:

_____

_____

_____

_____

How I plan to act on the sign/message:

_____

_____

_____

_____

Date
_____

What I saw/heard/felt:
_____

_____

_____

_____

What I sense it meant:
_____

_____

_____

_____

How it made me feel:
_____

_____

_____

_____

How I plan to act on the sign/message:
_____

_____

_____

_____

Date

What I saw/heard/felt:

What I sense it meant:

How it made me feel:

How I plan to act on the sign/message:

Date _____

What I saw/heard/felt:

_____

_____

_____

_____

What I sense it meant:

_____

_____

_____

_____

How it made me feel:

_____

_____

_____

_____

How I plan to act on the sign/message:

_____

_____

_____

_____

Date

What I saw/heard/felt:

What I sense it meant:

How it made me feel:

How I plan to act on the sign/message:

Index